FRESHWATER FOOD CHAINS

by Rebecca Pettiford

pogo

Ideas for Parents and Teachers

Pogo Books let children practice reading informational text while introducing them to nonfiction features such as headings, labels, sidebars, maps, and diagrams, as well as a table of contents, glossary, and index.

Carefully leveled text with a strong photo match offers early fluent readers the support they need to succeed.

Before Reading

- "Walk" through the book and point out the various nonfiction features. Ask the student what purpose each feature serves.
- Look at the glossary together. Read and discuss the words.

Read the Book

- Have the child read the book independently.
- Invite him or her to list questions that arise from reading.

After Reading

- Discuss the child's questions. Talk about how he or she might find answers to those questions.
- Prompt the child to think more. Ask: What other freshwater animals and plants do you know about? What food chains do you think they are a part of?

Pogo Books are published by Jump!
5357 Penn Avenue South
Minneapolis, MN 55419
www.jumplibrary.com

Library of Congress Cataloging-in-Publication Data

Names: Pettiford, Rebecca, author.
Title: Freshwater food chains / by Rebecca Pettiford.
Description: Minneapolis, MN: Jump!, Inc. [2016]
Series: Who eats what? | Audience: Ages 7-10.
Includes index.
Identifiers: LCCN 2016030809 (print)
LCCN 2016031651 (ebook)
ISBN 9781620315750 (hardcover: alk. paper)
ISBN 9781620316146 (pbk.)
ISBN 9781624965234 (ebook)
Subjects: LCSH: Food chains (Ecology)—Juvenile
literature. | Aquatic ecology—Juvenile literature.
Aquatic animals—Food—Juvenile literature.
Classification: LCC QH541.14 .P49 2016 (print)
LCC QH541.14 (ebook) | DDC 577.160916/9–dc23
LC record available at https://lccn.loc.gov/2016030809

Editor: Jenny Fretland VanVoorst
Book Designer: Michelle Sonnek
Photo Researcher: Michelle Sonnek

Photo Credits: All photos by Shutterstock except:
Alamy, 10-11, 19; Getty, 9, 12-13; iStock, 16-17;
SuperStock, 14-15, 20-21tm, 20-21bm, 20-21b.

Printed in the United States of America at
Corporate Graphics in North Mankato, Minnesota.

TABLE OF CONTENTS

CHAPTER 1

SALT-FREE WATER

Freshwater **biomes** are all over the world. They include lakes, ponds, rivers, and streams.

In rivers and streams, the water flows.

In ponds and lakes, the water is still. Unlike the ocean, freshwater biomes have very little salt. They have less than one percent!

Many plants and animals live in a freshwater **habitat**. Some live in the water. Others live or hunt along the bank.

Many insects live around lakes and ponds where the water is still. A lot of freshwater animals eat them. There is plenty to eat!

DID YOU KNOW?

Freshwater habitats are important to humans. Why? More than half of the water we drink comes from a freshwater habitat.

CHAPTER 2

THE FRESHWATER FOOD CHAIN

All living things need energy to grow. Food is energy. Freshwater plants use water and the sun to make their own food. Animals eat plants and other animals.

A **food chain** shows how energy moves from plants to animals. Each living link in the chain eats the one before it.

beaver
(consumer)

plants
(producers)

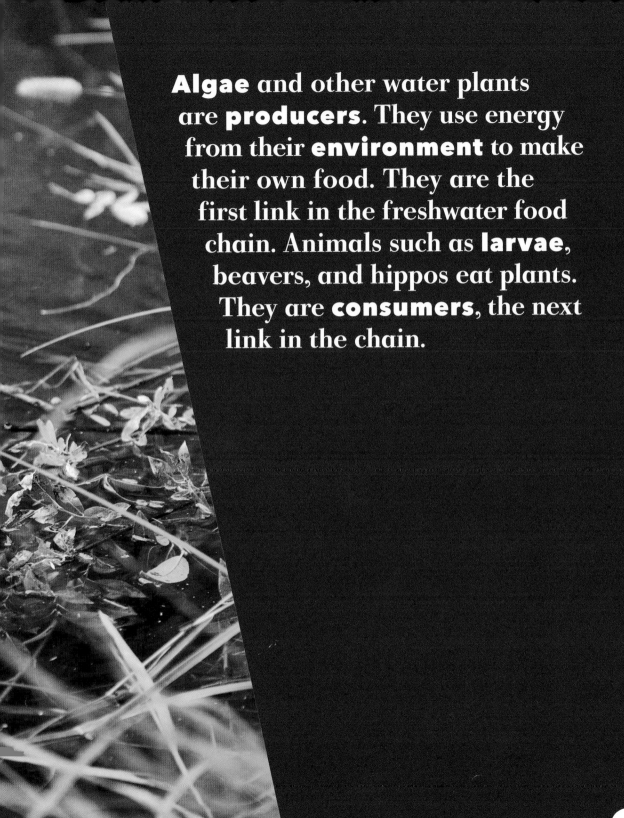

Algae and other water plants are **producers**. They use energy from their **environment** to make their own food. They are the first link in the freshwater food chain. Animals such as **larvae**, beavers, and hippos eat plants. They are **consumers**, the next link in the chain.

Predators are the next link in the food chain. They include frogs, birds, otters, and alligators.

Large predators will also eat smaller predators. For example, an alligator will eat an otter.

DID YOU KNOW?

Do not mess with river otters! They may look cute, but they are tough predators. Alligators eat them. But they have been known to kill and eat alligators as well!

alligator
(predator)

otter
(predator)

Food chains can be **complex**. Insects are **prey** for birds and small mammals. But many insects are also predators. Giant diving beetles eat tadpoles and other small water animals. Dragonfly larvae eat tadpoles. Then, when tadpoles grow into frogs, they eat dragonflies!

DID YOU KNOW?

When they feel danger, diving beetles give off a bad smell. It helps keep them from being eaten.

When an animal or plant dies, **bacteria**, flies, and **fungi** break it down. They are **decomposers**, the last link in the chain. The dead matter returns to the habitat as **nutrients**. The food chain continues.

A pond food chain might look something like this:

Producer: Tree

Predator: Otter

Consumer: Beaver

Decomposer: Bacteria

CHAPTER 3

FOOD CHAIN CLOSE-UPS

Let's look at a lake food chain. This one starts with a water plant. A snail eats the plant.

A **limpkin** eats the snail.
In time, the limpkin dies.
Bacteria break down its body.
The food chain begins again.

Let's look at a river food chain.

1) This one starts with algae.

2) A larva eats the algae.

3) A salmon eats the larva.

4) A bear eats the salmon.

One day, the bear dies.
Worms break down its body.
The food chain continues!

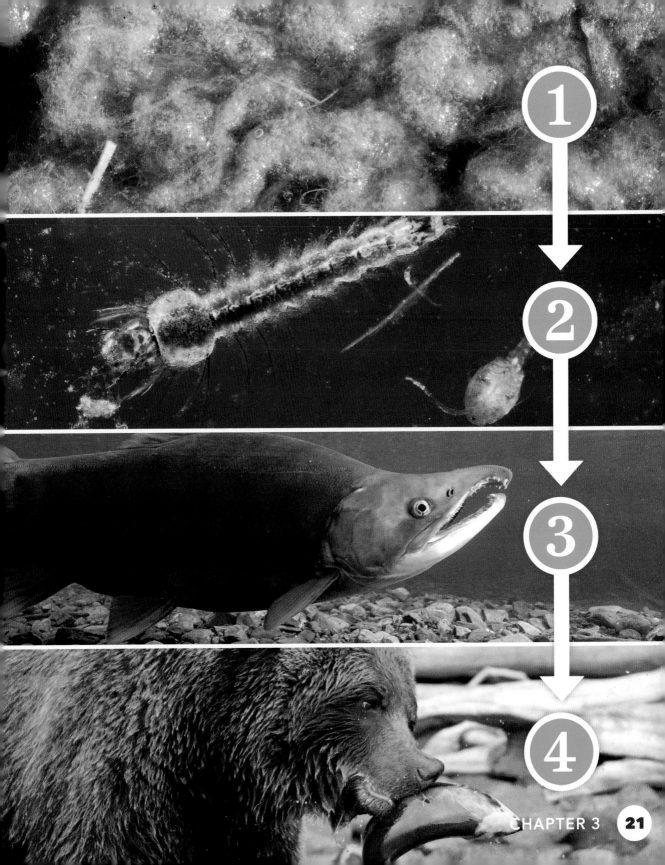

ACTIVITIES & TOOLS

TRY THIS!

STUDY A FRESHWATER HABITAT

Ponds, lakes, rivers, and streams provide homes for many different kinds of plants, animals, and insects. There is a good chance you live near a freshwater habitat. Grab a pencil and a notepad. Visit a freshwater pond, river, stream, or lake in your area. Do the following:

1. List the plants you see.

2. List the animals you see. Do not forget the insects!

3. How do the plants and animals depend on or use each other?

4. How do you think this freshwater home changes in the winter? In the summer?

GLOSSARY

algae: A plant that grows in the water; it does not have flowers, stems, roots, or leaves.

bacteria: Tiny life forms that break down dead plants and animals.

biomes: Large areas on Earth defined by their weather, land, and the type of plants and animals that live there.

complex: Having many parts, details, ideas, or functions, often related in a complicated way.

consumers: Animals that eat plants.

decomposers: Life forms that break down dead matter.

environment: All the factors (such as soil, climate, and living things) that surround a plant or animal and affect its survival.

food chain: An ordering of plants and animals in which each uses or eats the one before it for energy.

fungi: Living things, such as molds, that have no leaves, flowers, or roots and live on plant or animal matter.

habitat: The natural home or environment of an animal or plant.

larvae: The newly hatched, wingless form of many insects.

limpkin: A large wetland bird that lives in warm parts of the Americas.

nutrients: Substances that are essential for living things to survive and grow.

predators: Animals that hunt and eat other animals.

prey: Animals that are hunted and eaten by other animals.

producers: Plants that make their own food from the sun.

INDEX

TO LEARN MORE

Learning more is as easy as 1, 2, 3.

1) Go to www.factsurfer.com

2) Enter "freshwaterfoodchains" into the search box.

3) Click the "Surf" button to see a list of websites.

With factsurfer, finding more information is just a click away.